"I have told you these things, so that in me you may have peace. In this world you will have trouble. But take heart! I have overcome the world."

John 16:33 NIV

Oaklynn, Barrett David, and Houston,
May you always chase adventure and live with courage.
Make your dreams come true!
Love, Momma

Copyright © 2022

All rights reserved. This book or any portion thereof
may not be reproduced or used in any manner whatsoever
without the expressed written permission of the publisher
except for the use of brief quotations in a book review.
Printed in the United States of America
Editor: Christina Cawrse
ISBN: 979-8-218-06740-3
To Hope Publishing
First Printing, 2022
www.FromHurtToHope.com

Coco is curious and kind,
and has a lot on her mind.
When Coco wakes up each day she never knows what she will find.
She isn't really sure what she was made to do, but hopes and
prays her dreams will come true.
"I'm not sure what today will hold, but I'm excited to see.
Will you go on this journey with me?"

Just in that moment, Coco gets distracted when she sees friends out and about in the community.

"We have places to go and people to see, dreams to make into reality."

Coco loves to explore and rushes out the door.

"Everyone seems to have a mission in mind, I guess I'll figure out mine in time. Look at these trees and buzzing bees. No need to rush, there's nowhere better to be."

Coco moves too fast and passes the directions and warnings.

"I'll follow everyone else, they must know where they're going."

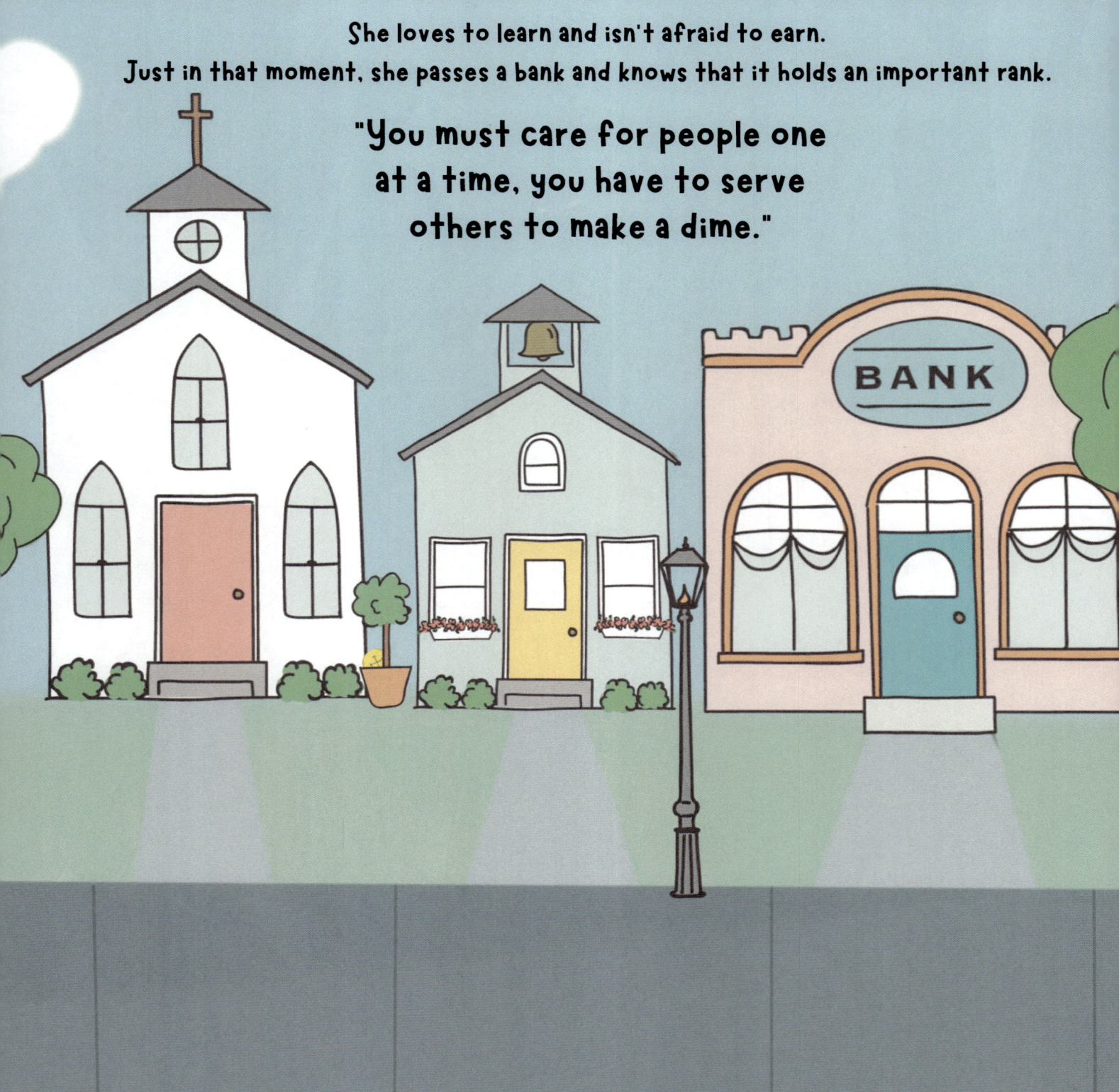

While out on her adventure of the day, she started to get a little hungry.

She passes the fruit stand and runs right to the cute stand.

Not thinking about the choices she makes, they really start to add up when made day after day.

Just at that moment Coco spots a group of "friends."
She hopes they will invite her to join them.

Coco's feelings are hurt by their words of dirt.

She's only trying to help, and never to hurt.

"People don't see things the way that I do, they make me feel crazy, maybe it's true. I'm just trying to help others. I can't help that I dream, I feel like I have a purpose, why can't they see that in me?"

At just the moment when things were getting too dark to see, a light caught her eye and reflected off of something very shiny.

Coco climbs down from the tree, she has to see what this is all about. After all, she is very lost from wandering about.

"How did this happen? How can this be?
How did I find a compass in my time of most need?"

When she finds the compass she knows things are about to change.
She feels happiness and peace for the first time today.

"I'm not sure how this is possible!

I must tell everyone I see.

The compass I just found

is really going to help me!"

People can't believe that she actually came back, little did they know that it was just an attack.

She found the truth while away for a while and knows she now has a reason to smile.

"I want to share with you what I found, a compass that helped me when I got lost and turned around. It helped me make my way back home, and now I know that I am never alone."

Everyone gathers around to hear more of the story. She forgives them for what they said, because she does not want to live a life of dread.

No one is perfect, not a single one in the crowd. We have to love one another in quiet and out loud.

She smiles at them and reaches out her hand, she wants to share what she's found with everyone she can.
She knows in her heart that this will be the best part.

Now it's time for the real adventure to start!

Here is a compass of your very own!
You never have to go on this journey alone!

Made in the USA
Middletown, DE
23 September 2022